THE STORIES OF ATHENS

Ancient History 5th Grade
Children's Ancient History

Known as one of the greatest cities throughout the world, it became the center of art, philosophy and power throughout the world during the era of the Ancient Greeks. In this book, we will be learning the history of this great city.

Athens - The Oldest City

With a history that is recorded back 3400 years, Athens is also one of the oldest cities around the world. It is known as the heart of Ancient Greek Civilization and the birthplace of democracy.

STATUE OF ATHENA

Named after Athena

A thens was named for Athena, the Greek goddess who was the goddess of civilization, wisdom, and war as well as the patron of Athens. The Parthenon, which is her shrine, can be found atop a hill located in the center of Athens.

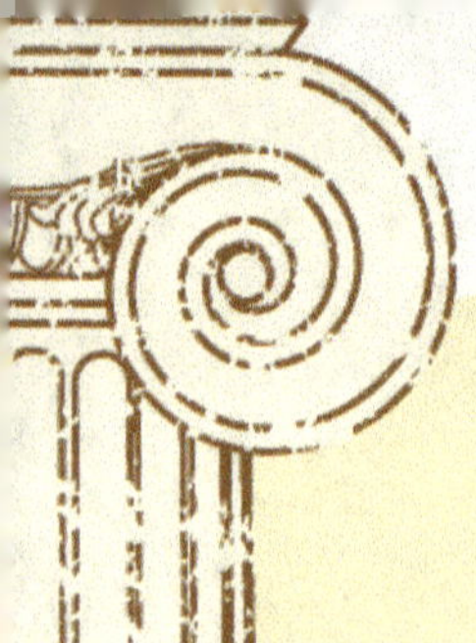

The Agora

This was the center of government and commerce in ancient Athens. There was a huge open area that was used for meetings and this area was surrounded by buildings. Several of these buildings were temples that included temples build for Apollo, Hephaestus, and Zeus. Some buildings were government buildings such as the Strategeion, where the Strategoi (10 military leaders of Athens) would meet, and the Mint, where they made coins.

ANCIENT AGORA, ATHENS

ENTRANCE TO THE AGORA

This became a meeting place for people to gather and discuss their ideas and beliefs about government and philosophy, and is considered to be the place were ancient Greece democracy first came to life.

The Acropolis

The Acropolis was constructed in the Middle of Athens on a hill. It was surrounded by walls of stone and was built originally to be a fortress and citadel where people could retreat when there was an attack on the city. Several buildings and temples were constructed later overlooking the city. However, it continued to be used as a fortress for some time.

ERECHTHEUM

The Parthenon is located at the center of the Acropolis and was dedicated to Athena as well as being used for storing gold. The Erchtheum and the Temple of Athena Nike are other temples that are located here.

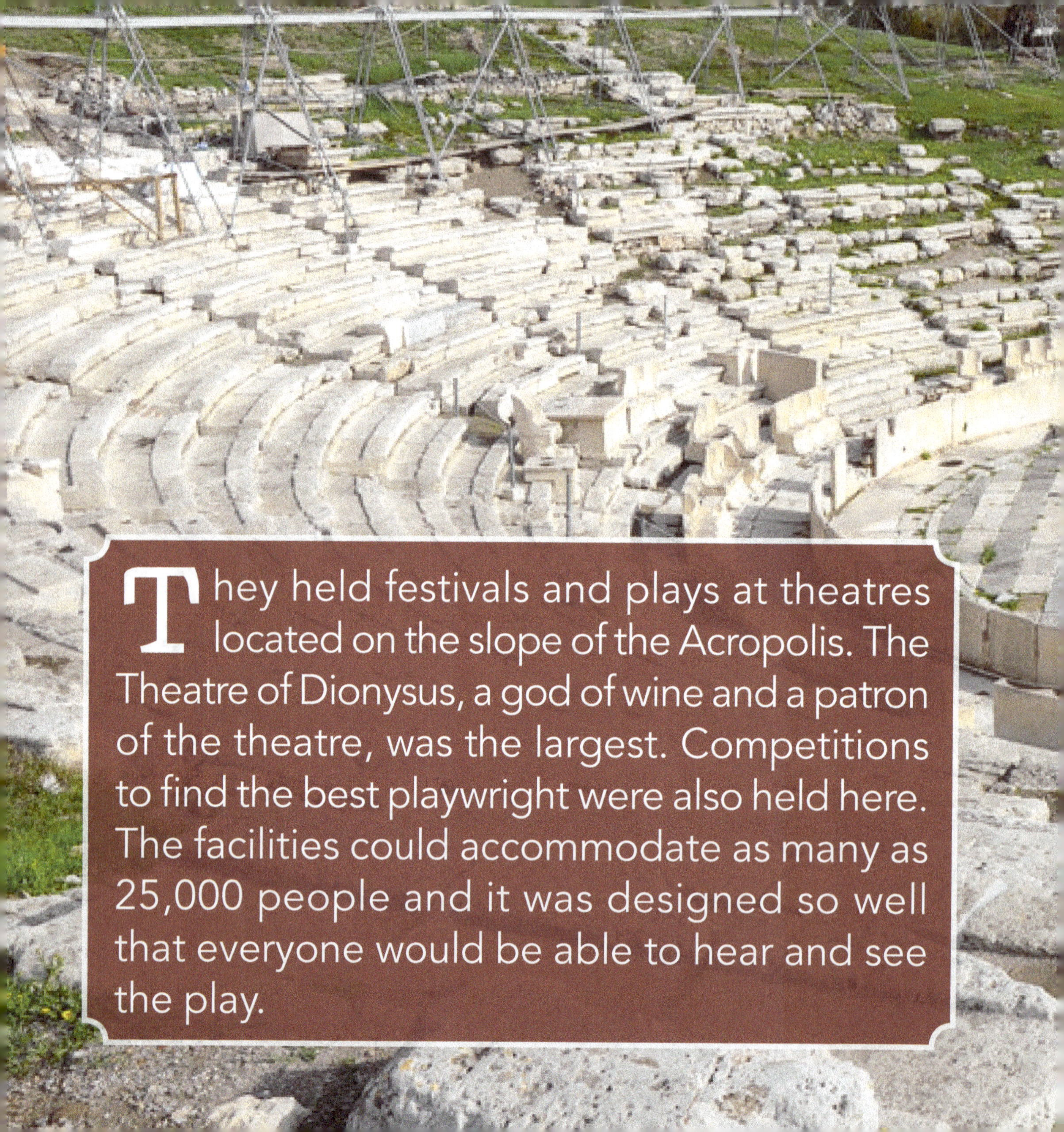

They held festivals and plays at theatres located on the slope of the Acropolis. The Theatre of Dionysus, a god of wine and a patron of the theatre, was the largest. Competitions to find the best playwright were also held here. The facilities could accommodate as many as 25,000 people and it was designed so well that everyone would be able to hear and see the play.

THEATRE OF DIONYSUS

PERICLES

The Age of Pericles

Ancient Athens came to its peak during Pericles leadership, from 461 to 429 BC, which was known as the Age of Pericles. It was during this era that the literature, the arts, and democracy were promoted. In addition, he built several of Athens' amazing structures, which included building the Parthenon and rebuilding most of Acropolis.

Athena

Athena is a Greek goddess and is one of the Twelve Olympians. Most known for being the god of Athens, she also assisted several of the Greek heroes, including Odysseus and Hercules, throughout their adventures.

Often depicted to be a warrior armed with a shield, helmet, and spear, she would sometimes be seen wearing a cloak or a shield that was adorned with the head of Medusa, a monster.

STATUE OF ATHENA

PALLAS ATHENA BY REMBRANDT

What Were Her Skills and Powers?

Similar to the rest of the Olympians, Athena was a goddess that was immortal and she could not die. In addition, she was one of the more wisest and intelligent of the Greek gods and was known to be great at war strategy and providing heroes with courage.

She also had the ability to create useful crafts and items. She was the inventor of the chariot, the ship, the rake, and the plow as well as inventing many skills utilized by women in Ancient Greece, including pottery and weaving.

GREEK VASE

ZEUS

Athena's Birth

Athena was born to the leader of Zeus, the god leader of the Olympians and Metis, who was a Titan. Even though Zeus was married to Metis, he was afraid of her power. He overheard a prophesy one day that one of her children would take over Zeus' throne. He quickly swallowed Metis and believed that the problem was now solved.

Zeus was unaware that Metis was pregnant with Athena when he swallowed her. She gave birth to Athena inside of Zeus and created a spear, shield, and helmet. While Athena continued to grow inside of his head, he got a terrible headache. He could no longer stand it and eventually had the god named Hephaestus crack his head open with an ax. Athena then jumped out of his head. She was fully grown and she was armed with a spear and a shield.

STATUE OF HEPHAESTUS

Protector of the City of Athens

After she won a contest along with the god Poseidon, Athena became the city of Athens' patron goddess. Each god would present a gift to the city. Poseidon created the horse and presented it to Athens. Athena created the olive tree and presented it to the city. Even though both gifts were considered useful, the people of Athens felt that the olive tree was a more valuable gift and made Athena their patron.

Athena was honored by the people of Athens by building the big acropolis located in the city's center. They build a gorgeous temple to Athena at the top of the acropolis and named it the Parthenon.

STATUE OF HERCULES

Assisting the Heroes

Athena is also famous for assisting the heroes when on their adventures. She assisted Hercules with achieving his twelve labors, she helped Perseus figure out how he could defeat Medusa, she helped Odysseus with his adventures at the Odyssey, as well as helping Jason build the Argo, his magical ship.

Arachne

In Greek mythology, Athena created weaving and was known to be the best. However, one day, Arachne, who was the daughter of a shepherd, claimed that she was the best. Athena became angry about this and visited Arachne, challenging her to a contest. When the weaving contest started, Athena created a weaving with a picture of how mortals were punished by the gods for their claims of being equals. Arachne created a woven picture of how the gods interfered with the mortals and played with their lives.

ARACHNE

ATHENA CHANGING ARACHNE INTO A SPIDER

O nce the contest came to an end, Athena became angry once she saw Arachne's weaving. Not only was this weaving better than hers, it portrayed the gods in a foolish way. Athena cursed at Arachne and turned her into a spider.

Pericles

Pericles was raised at the time of the Persian Wars. When he was about three, Athens was facing their first major assault by the Persians, but were victorious at the Battle of Marathon. Athens would again face the Persians ten years later and they left the city this time and most of Athens was destroyed by the Persians. However, they were able to defeat the Persians during the Battle of Salamis and Pericles returned home.

BATTLE OF SALAMIS

AESCHYLUS

Pericles started using his wealth in support of the arts when he was a young man. One of the first items on his list was sponsoring Aeschylus, a playwright, and his play The Persians, which told of Athens defeating the Persians during the Battle of Salamis. This was a successful play and Pericles was becoming a popular man in Athens.

His Early Career in Politics

Pericles decided to take on Areopagus, a powerful council of leaders, in his early political career. Along with his allies, he assisted in stripping the power from these men. This became an important part of democracy's history. He became more popular with the citizens of Athens and would move on to the forefront of politics in Athens.

THE AREOPAGUS IN ATHENS

AMPHITHEATRE AT DELPHI CITY

Military Expeditions

Pericles went on to become the stragegos, otherwise known as a general, of the Athenian army and led many military campaigns that were a success. He helped in taking control of the city of Delphi from the Spartans and also was able to conquer the Thracian peninsula located in Gallipoli and was able to establish an Athenian colony in that location.

Laws and Politics

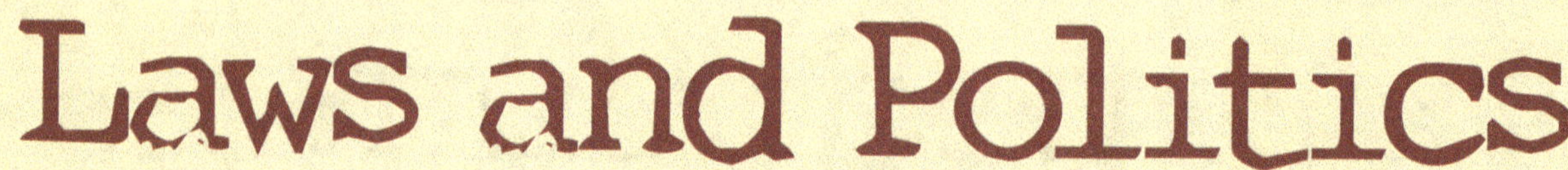

In addition, Pericles worked on restructuring the Athenian democracy by introducing new ideas and laws. One such law was that a person sitting on a jury should be paid for this service. While this may seem like a simple law, it allowed for a poor person to sit on a jury, which only the rich could afford taking off work and serving on a jury previously.

ACROPOLIS OF ATHENS

Building Projects

Pericles is probably most famous for his amazing building projects. His desire was establishing Athens as leader of the Greek world and his wish was to build an acropolis representing the glory of Athens. He rebuilt several of the temples on the acropolis that the Persians had destroyed. Additionally, he had the Long Walls constructed from Athens to Piraeus to protect it should a siege take place.

The Parthenon was his most famous project on the acropolis. This amazing structure was a temple to Athena and was constructed between 447 BC and 438 BC, taking more than 20 thousand tons of marble to build.

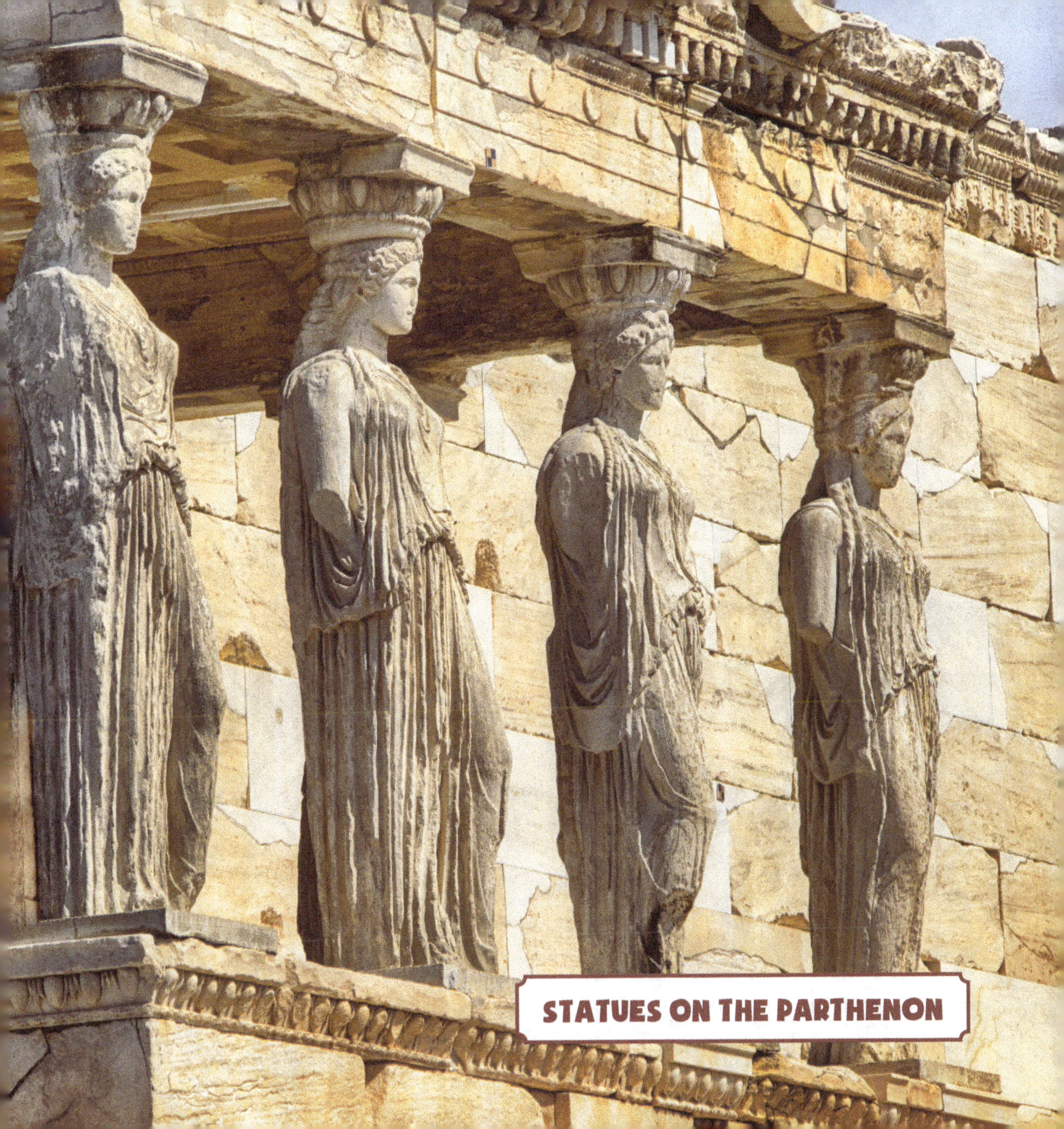

STATUES ON THE PARTHENON

MARBLE STATUE OF THE ANCIENT PHILOSOPHER SOCRATES

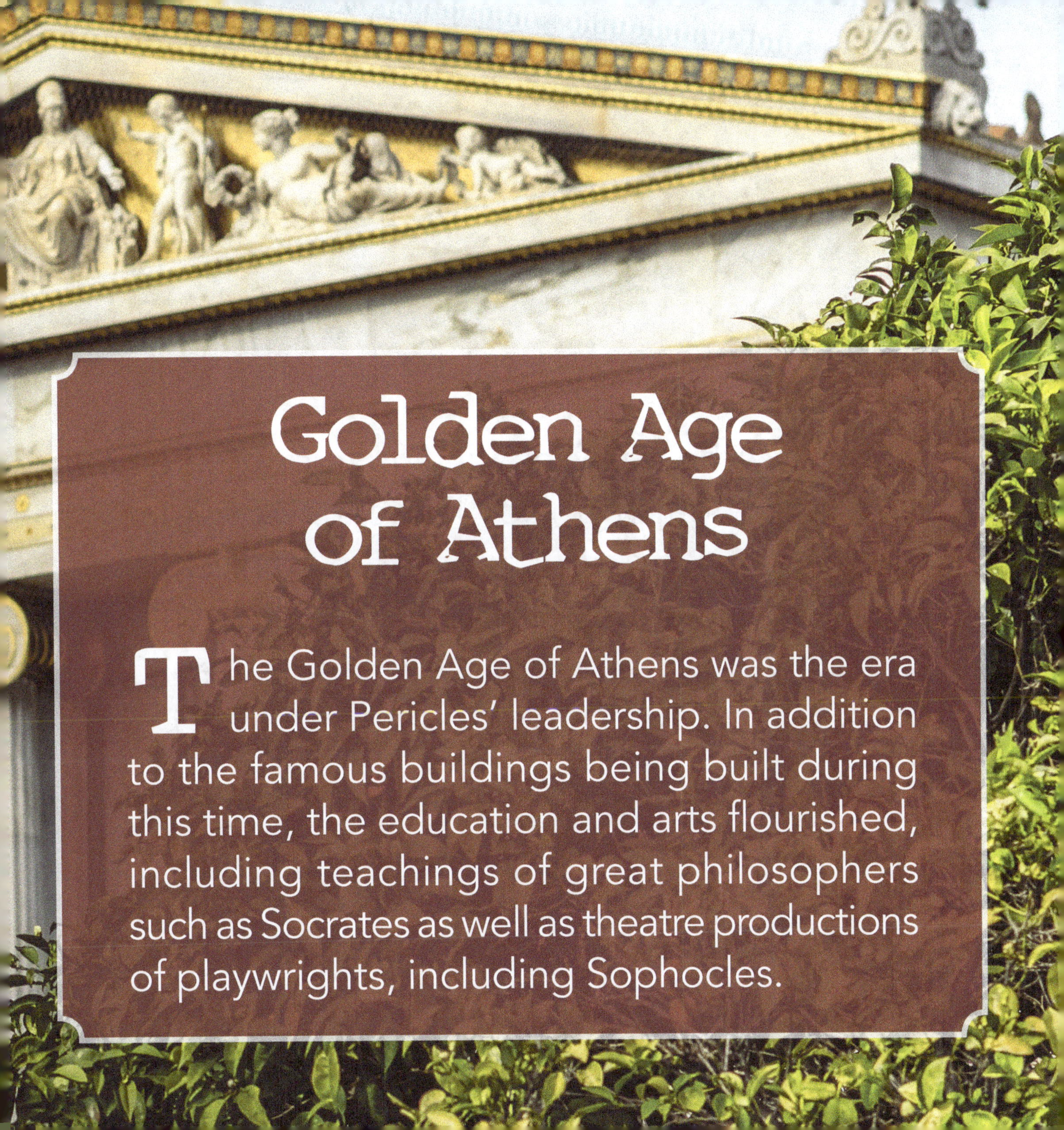

Golden Age of Athens

The Golden Age of Athens was the era under Pericles' leadership. In addition to the famous buildings being built during this time, the education and arts flourished, including teachings of great philosophers such as Socrates as well as theatre productions of playwrights, including Sophocles.

War with Sparta

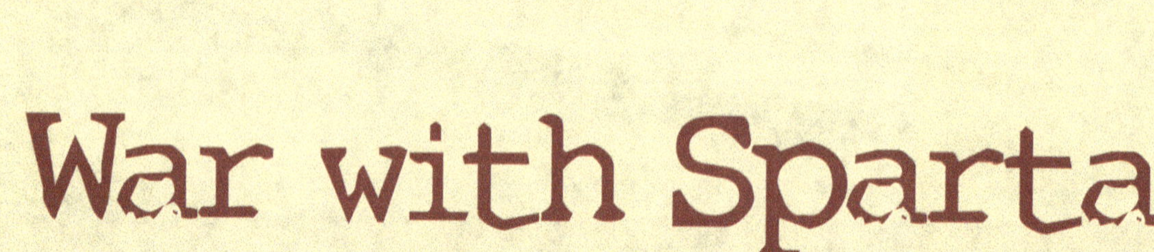

While Athens was continuing to grow in power and wealth under Pericles' leadership, the other Greek city-states were starting to be concerned, as they felt Athens was becoming too powerful. The war between Athens and Sparta, known as the Peloponnesian War, began in 431 BC.

SPARTAN SOLDIER

Funeral Oration

Shortly after the beginning of the Peloponnesian War, Pericles gave the Funeral Oration, which became famous. This speech was to honor soldiers that already had died. In his speech, Pericles presented the ideals and democracy of Athens. The speech was memorialized in writing and is one way that historians are able to describe how people of Athens felt.

The Plague

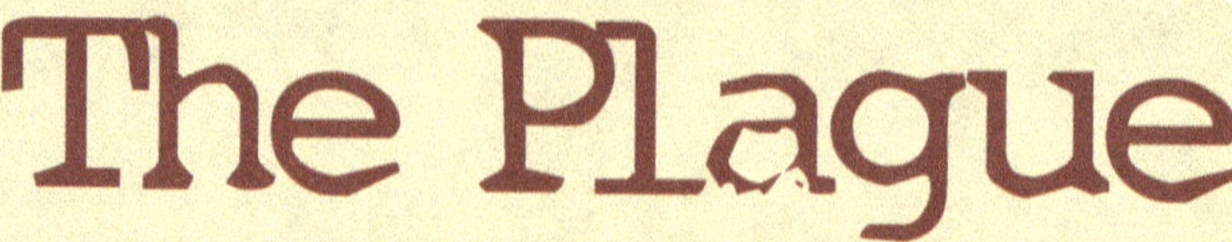

Pericles' approach to fight Sparta was fighting at sea, not land. Athens had the stronger navy, however, Sparta had the stronger army. The citizens of Athens congregated in the city and had the Long Walls that stretched to the port enabling them to obtain any supplies they needed. While this approach might have worked, Athens was struck by a plague and thousands perished. Pericles also died in 429 BC from the plague. Eventually, Athens lost the war and was never able to recover.

Athens is only a small part of the history and mystery surrounding Greek mythology. For additional information, you can visit your local library, research the internet, and ask questions of your teachers, family, and friends.

Visit
BABY PROFESSOR
EDUCATION KIDS
www.BabyProfessorBooks.com
to download Free Baby Professor eBooks
and view our catalog of new and exciting
Children's Books